SEAM

PROSE POEMS

Seam *(noun):*

1. the line where two or more layers of fabric are held together by stitches
2. a bed or a distinct layer or vein of rock in other layers of rock
3. a supply of something valuable
4. a trace or presence of something

Seam: Prose Poems
Recent Work Press
Canberra

Poems © the authors 2015

Second Edition
ISBN 978-0-9944565-9-5
Editor: Shane Strange

All rights reserved. This book is copyright. Except for private study, research, criticism or reviews as permitted under the Copyright Act, no part of this book may be reproduced, stored in a retrieval system, or transmitted in any form by any means without prior written permission. Enquiries should be addressed to the publisher.

This book made possible with the support of:

International Poetry Studies Institute
Faculty of Arts and Design
University of Canberra
Canberra, Australia
http://ipsi.org.au

Design: Caren Florance
www.ampersandduck.com

Cover image from *The Iron and Steel Magazine*, 1898. "*Fig 3 ... represent[s] a batch of rails which mashed down in a few months upon another road to the contour represented by the dotted line. The unbroken line represents the template, and the large black areas indicate holes in the steel which were formed by the elongation of the metal upon the top of the rail when the failure began...*" http://tinyurl.com/qyu5h5

recentworkpress.com

SEAM

PROSE POEMS

by the Prose Poetry Project
Edited by Shane Strange

CONTENTS

History	9
Touch	13
Domestic	17
Practice	21
Testament	25
Adaptation	29
Make	33
Words	37
Resignation	41
Navigation	45
Walk	49
Professional	53
Lost	57
Animal	61
Remnant	65
Art	69
Doors	73
Room	77
Regret	81
Care	85
Ophelia	89

INTRODUCTION

As of this writing, the Prose Poetry Project has grown from three poets from the International Poetry Studies Institute (IPSI), based at the University of Canberra, to include 17 contributing writers from universities across Australia and the UK, who have between them written some 650 prose poems since November 2014. This is a significant resource often produced in swirling intensities of composition where ideas, phrases, or suggestions are responded to, inflected, reinterpreted, and represented—much like when a collective musical improvisation coalesces around a certain phrasing or run of notes, before skittering away again to find new combinations, interpretations, and ways of doing. In editing this volume I was aware that I could only give the briefest hint to the reader of what this process is like. So I chose instead to 'mine' the project, selecting pairs of prose poems to align under a specific theme. In this way I hope to show my sense of two prose poems speaking to each other: joining in conversation; or speaking to the same thing in unison; or separated by a period of time, riffing on the same theme, the same word even, yet still finding coincidence in my perception of their harmony.

While this is an intimate setting for these works, I hope in presenting this thin sliver to give a taste of the richness of the project as a whole. In other words, this necessarily concise and highly subjective selection does not do justice to the rich life of the project. Nevertheless, for the moment, it has to suffice.

– *Shane Strange, August, 2015*

With this second edition, reissued by Recent Work Press, thanks are due to Caren Florance for her original design and layout, to the poets for their (contintuing) collaboration, and to the the International Poetry Studies Institute (IPSI), part of the Centre for Creative and Cultural Research, Faculty of Arts and Design, University of Canberra for their ongoing support.

– *Shane Strange, July, 2016*

HISTORY

We were in Berlin, at the Libeskind, when the corridors faded out, when the walls closed in. You walked me into the murders of history, you stole everything I owned. In Johannesburg, on the pavement outside the cinema, a man slumped against a shop, bleeding. My father held him as he died. I have hidden my copy of the Goya print inside my atlas; it contains events I still can't discuss. Auden warned us, but who listened? In Manchester, at the Libeskind, all the lights went out and the room turned red, and over the intercom a man spoke in German. It was last century when Nietzsche collapsed, when Althusser ran crazy through the streets. The authorities erected concrete bollards there. Keeping the philosophers at bay. The architects have gone into hiding, the artists are in hiding, the poets still slink through the laneways, chasing ambulances, seeing what no one should ever see.

Jen Webb

One year and nine months and he has not stopped moving—places you were together and ones intended. In his pocket, zip-lock bags of you, small rubble, gritty dust, uncompromising as in life. You have been snatched by the wind at Machu Picchu, furtively dumped at Gracelands, have accreted the fields of Civil War dead and fallen noiseless and twisting from the cliffs at Royal. Today you anoint Karl Marx's grave at Highgate (also the bust of Bruce Reynolds, mastermind of the Great Train Robbery, but not the cool, shadowed plinth of George Eliot). The historian in you would be tickled, I think. Resting on a bench crocheted with lichen, by the plain stone of Sidney Nolan, he says, you should really talk about this stuff. We didn't. Next week he takes you to Auschwitz.

Penelope Layland

TOUCH

The weight of a certain memory from a time ago; his nails pressed into her palm and a voice not quite her own saying softly it's enough. Later, cockling would remind her of their hands clasped together in this way; the anticipation of a small hunt on the day their dogs walked the bar with them out to the deep seams in soft wet sand, placing their feet as carefully as horses, and how the search sometimes unexpectedly hurt her hands. To the side of her one of her sisters gone mad with the plenty of her patch, and then her patient brother's plea: *basta, amore,* enough! In the bucket the shells sat closed tight inside their own pearlescent mysteries. Later, in the pan, they would open like one hand releasing another, a softness divulged from a shelf of hardness. She had lifted her head from his shoulder and curled inside that movement lay his unloosed grip, as if this originary contact might contain the fossil of all future embraces. And despite the knowledge she had foraged from somewhere in deep, the dog's and her brother's warnings to walk carefully and not take too much, she knew from that point on nothing would ever be enough.

Lucy Dougan

Touch evokes a room where now forgotten words were hung like clothes. Where we lay in semi-dark as metaphor re-entered neglected speech. Where, barely seen, we were puzzlingly known—or unknown, but persuaded of ourselves. Whatever belonged there did not belong; we borrowed facsimiles of other emotions in order to know our feelings better. We belonged to scent, taste, hearing, touch. Opacity was a warm tide; skin-flush; an escapade. We stood away from ourselves and, leaving, knew what only skin knows.

Paul Hetherington

DOMESTIC

Breakfast civility. Bone china cups, saucers, plates, and a silver toast rack—its ribcage of yellowing tusks like tapered candles that have softened, drooped, curled right over. Then hardened. You listen to a scraping of knives. You listen harder—lean in to take a closer look, lean too close and civility breaks with a wild boar scream—a scream that pulses from another time, another place. You're blameless in the thick of pulsing screams. A bone-handled knife presses into the palm of your blameless, pulsing, scraping hand.

Paul Munden

The knives in the cupboard drawer haunted her dreams. She imagined them lying together, like a family that could slice itself up: hard edged, sharp witted, good at cutting up love into bite-sized chunks, good at cutting skin or soft fruit. The knife with the serrated edge reminded her of her mother and she could not quite pin-point why. Something to do with gutting and bread, loaves and fishes. The ability to produce a meal out of nothing. Small miracles, night after night served up on china plates printed with chintz. She would sharpen the knives tomorrow after work. Keep them clean and in working order. All that gleaming Sheffield steel in the dark drawer lined with green felt.

Anne Caldwell

PRACTICE

He was digging down, all the way to Australia, it can't be worse than here, he thought; the quartz sand gave way to crushed sea shell, fossiliferous shale and strata of sedimentary rock, an outcrop of Upper Ordovician limestone halted his progress momentarily; and then drifting in, on an offshore breeze, he could hear the dreams and strange songlines that were etched in the coal seams, nouns like vistas, rivers of sayings, stories as ancient as the earth; the tide reached back up the beach and filled the hole he had dug, tomorrow he would begin again, perhaps not quite as close to the sea...

Andrew Melrose

I used to trust the system, but year by year they've beaten it out of me. All those affidavits, the estoppels, ratios and dicta. None of it makes any sense. And year by fucking year it happens again: the unreasonable ruling from the high court, the swift justice, mothers in tears, the torn garments.

Practice makes perfect. We are learning to infuse the annual anguish with a lighter note. One day we'll get it right.

Yesterday we decorated a dozen eggs and rolled them down the hill. Fewer than half cracked—it felt like success. We gathered up the shells, we stacked them before the mouth of the cave. They'll be safe there: no one ever rolls the stone away.

Jen Webb

TESTAMENT

When we saw the small sculptures, evening had distorted all sense of distance. It was as if we could hold out hands and haul them towards us—and one in the party tried to do just that. We ate at a tavern where the proprietor kept shaking his head; his rissoles were dry and burnt. We washed sand from faces, and dust from throats with pungent, unspeakable wine. The next morning, eating breakfast, we could see them through a window—not sculptures but upright crosses; figures that seemed pegged there. We'd not known the war had come this far. Although it was early we were served more wine, swilling its sour redolence in our mouths.

Paul Hetherington

Gaudi himself saw in leaf shapes and the force of gravity his own genius for tiling. And in mushroom chimney pots, the onset of modernity, to be kept at bay by the construction of half a cathedral. It was there that I sat across from his lifeless 'The Slaughter of the Innocents' while my own son, with frothing mouth and bag filled with orange piss, lay in a local hospital, near death. Through tears I asked, can this cup be passed from me, but the response was a canvas sack dangling pendulum-like over the great architect's office desk: the simulacrum of his final uneaten meal. Great architect, I thought, vulgar and unlucky, no matter how beggarly you dressed, even you could not escape the forces that fix us to the inevitable.

Shane Strange

ADAPTATION

Last night I pressed my body to the cold tiles on the bathroom floor. Face down. Recumbent. Prone. To making mistakes. My torso left a hot patch beneath the vanity basin. When you came to find me I had misted up the mirror with my heat. I shifted sideways to find fresh tiles while you wrote Tennessee Williams on the steamy glass. You stepped into my hot spot. Toes curling into the warmth. 'Listen,' you said, 'can you hear it?' Somewhere in my imagination a streetcar still grinds its way down Desire Street. Even though we both know it has been retired. Retrenched. Put to sleep. And now you will have to rely on the bus to take you to your Elysian Field. I turned my head to the left and stared at the sock line circumnavigating your ankle. You shaved in the double 'e' of Tennessee and called me your *Belle Reve. Tristes tropiques.* I blanched and peeled myself off the floor. Sticky sweat clinging to the white tiles. You looked for a moment at my flushed belly before taking the bottle of eye drops and tipping back your head, cap in mouth. Gagged. Censored. Silenced. Post-Katrina in the Crescent City and I'm still waiting for more levees to burst. Me with my Hurricane box watching *Treme* on HBO. You drinking Hurricanes at Old Absinthe House in the Vieux Carré. Toulouse Street. Toulouse-Lautrec. *La blanchisseuse.* 'Don't worry,' you told me once, 'it's only a paper moon.' But we both know it is only you who is sailing over the cardboard sea. I'm just papier-mâché. You chew me up and spit me out. Pulp. Palpitations. So I paste myself onto you. Moulding myself into your curves. But you don't wait for the glue to dry and so we rot from the inside out.

Cassandra Atherton

Lady Macduff, so beautiful, so young, is delaying proceedings; it's her first day, she's worried about her hair. There are whispers...Another ten minutes. Someone puts a red cross on the far, green wall. Thick wires spill from the camera like arteries. Finally, she reappears, her hair the same perfection it was before. I want to tell her how little it matters, but my presence means nothing. It's as if I'm not there. I'm not there.

Paul Munden

MAKE

as chekhov well knew, a whelk that is attached to the wall above the fireplace in the first verse must remain attached to the wall in the last verse, and indeed, even after the poem is over and the embers are burning down, the whelk should be left to its own devices—commonly, sliding from one edge to another in last search of the lost ocean, or fixed in place, turning in on the waves of its loss. under no circumstances should one try to fire the whelk; it is not a revolver, and though some species of snail may shoot 'dribbling darts of love', the whelk (in the right environment) reproduces by internal fertilisation. where an uncle is present he should not be allowed to cross to the hearth to finger the spiral; his translations are no help.

Jen Crawford

When he sat in restaurants Zac wrote poems on paper napkins. Poems were like the change in your pocket. Unlike Emily Dickinson, Zac wanted to escape into prose. When he'd first stepped into the *mansarda* in The Street of Perfect Love he'd felt compelled to write something that had little to do with poetry as he usually thought of it. He didn't have much patience for notions of automatic writing but he had to admit that there was a certain compulsion about his more recent literary endeavour. When he sat down at the long table in that large, sunlit apartment the typewriter hardly ever seemed to snag.

Julian Stannard

WORDS

They are not the rising inside of thighs, or the plosive capsules of some maker's words. The valley between is no unwinding of grammar. Yet, for a moment I imagine myself small as a pronoun; and this is the view a paragraph affords—as if I've been quietly let go by your tongue.

Paul Hetherington

Words they mouth. Sensing shapes of o and gee. Letters they mouth, bleeding tongues on w. Mouthing the first daffodils, the last mandarins. Mouths drying on old hairbrushes, tongue-tips working the pig-bristles up and flick. Close to ground mouths where move is eat eat, the world a tug-rope inching in in. Mouthing faces, sucking the slopes of nose to cheek. Hello Aunty. Thirsty searching for meaty leather, yolk, frosticles on the metal Moore thigh.

Monica Carroll

RESIGNATION

I'm superman. I fly through space, beat up the bad guys and make them surrender. But I can't seem to solve the arms problem or stop so many individuals owning guns, I guess because at bottom human nature likes to hurt others. I guess ultimately the answer is education, so I should get a B Ed. or something equivalent.

Owen Bullock

Mercator peeled the world like an orange and ironed out its skin. Africa diminished, Asia shrank, faded away. Do we still matter? Tonight nine people are locked in solitary cells. Soon they will reach for each other's hands, and turn to face the guns. There are no words for this. They are shadows already. While they wait, one finishes his painting, one turns to prayer. I pore over the documents, while the experts insist there is no way out, no hole that affords an escape. They wait, we wait, the world is not as it seems. Skin me, flatten out my skin. Weeping is all we have left.

Jen Webb

NAVIGATION

Maps from the fifteenth century are mostly blank page and bluntly rugged lines of coast that halt; gaps oblige the sea of kraken and hydra gushing onto charted land. Cartographers drew the line closed, forgetting to drain the ground of monsters. At night, the blind squid under my bed slimes a cracked tentacle down the hall, stealing cat biscuits and messing up the Lego. I ask it to sleep beside me, something real to cuddle. Our pillow talk is imagining the ways we could bind limbs, slip inside, choke breath and stop ears. I set out two bowls of biscuits and stroke its musculature in reach.

Monica Carroll

We play a game where each must sleep until we dream the sea. You shall be the fisher, I your amanuensis. You have travelled to Iceland, oiling the harpoons. My job is to mark the maps and burn them in the furnace. You say 'It requires the skill of the scuba!' I carve that into the mast. Our catch is slim, but our backs are bronze plate and peeling. I collect the scales to make paper. The journal of our voyage now reaches to eight volumes. I sew the nets, mark the Transit of Venus, the line of longitude. You sweat in the hammock, febrile, muttering 'Wranglers must venture far beyond, and later return in order to stand a chance.'

Shane Strange

WALK

As he walked past the busy bar, thoughts of elusive merriment lingered, but the murmured tones of Roy Orbison singing, 'Only the Lonely,' an ageing poet in search of beauty left an icy shard. He had no appetite for food, love, wine, the companionship of Falstaffian friends; after Basho his words lay like coffee grinds at the bottom of a paper cup, random stepping stones in a mess of brown sludge leaving no clues as to which way the narrative was heading.

Andrew Melrose

The narrative is walking through Europe towards Greece. It recently acquired a donkey, which gives the protagonist something to talk to. It began on the Comino, the sociable solitary and the feet, one, one and one, the sense of wandering. Heading east, the protagonist returns to New Zealand and Australia, but not before meeting a monk who wears Levis and tends the hooves of animals with an omniscient first person; a Welsh dance teacher who makes origami, speaking to the listener with their own speech mannerisms; an Indian cook who dices vegetables with the honesty of a teenager. The narrative is almost home now.

Owen Bullock

PROFESSIONAL

Mostly, you'll have to learn as you go. But here is information that might help you through the first days:

> Luck can fall from the sky. But don't presume that it's all good luck.
>
> The most popular song on the jukebox is something histrionic by Mister Roy Orbison.
>
> 'Shanti' is a word from an old Eastern scripture. Keep it available in your mind so it can serve your emotion.
>
> The client will presume that there is nothing here—NOTHING—that is banned from importuning. This is regardless of whether or not the thing has a name. I mean, some other name, different from 'thing'.
>
> There are nights when the rain hits the roof with a rhythm that's Cuban.
>
> If ordered to use the knife, go at the task just like it's regular chicken.

Ross Gibson

the social work intern is surprised that the youths must squat to greet visitors to the centre. the shock puts him in a sombre mood.

the social work intern has an immediate sense of the loss of dignity among the youths when he sees them squatting at toilets in full view of the staff.

the social work intern arranges a game of crab soccer. he wants to slow the youths' dynamics so he can observe them more closely. he's here to learn. everyone's on their hands and knees.

This poem uses language from 'Working with Reformative Trainees', by Myrle de Souza. Singapore: Juvenile Justice Department, Beyond Social Services, 2007. http://www.beyondresearch.sg/report/Thesis%20Myrle%20K.pdf

Jen Crawford

LOST

In a space that's the green of absence a man walks in sunlight. He's lost his glasses, wonders whether they're still on the train, nestled on vinyl after seeing the hills—an old property ensconced in trees. He and a friend, locating themselves. And now, through that lens, someone dreams of the landscape—nouns like vistas, rivers of saying.

Paul Hetherington

When I mislaid the diamond you gave me, you were unexpectedly serene. Not so when I lost the car keys, the book you were reading, your mother's phone number. Not so when I mislaid the map, dropped the fishing rod overboard, fell through the glass. For months we grappled with the inconstancy of things: nailing water to a board, drawing the blinds to arrest stray beams of light, summoning a storm. The hills above our house trembled, mud sluiced across the lawn, the sky roiled. No more magic. Our tongues lost the art of speech, our hands forgot how to touch, the tender interval between the notes shrank to a narrow bar. I kept losing things: my wallet, my watch, your heart. I forgot the way home.

Jen Webb

ANIMAL

The cows are obedient as they line up for the dip. Shitting in the mud where they stand, they move forward down the race: inch by inch to the edge. Two men with electric prods force the cows into the dipping trench: one by one by one. And the boy sees from the fence how they work as a machine: the line of cows; the men.

   The dip itself is milky blue and splashes across the yard as each cow jumps in. When the boy gets some on his skin his grandfather tells the boy to 'wipe it off quick' with his red handkerchief. The boy does as he's told. 'Chemicals,' his grandfather mumbles. But the boy is more concerned about the red handkerchief, and the bull in the yard next door, waiting, he has been told, to be neutered.

Shane Strange

Alice made a nest of coats in the caravan she borrowed from a friend. She was off grid, with no phone signal or T.V. It rained all night. Nidderdale rain, heavy and persistent, drumming on the metal roof of her box-shaped room, with the sound of the river like a base note in the music of water. Her father would have remarked, *it's raining stair rods, lass* or *raining cats and dogs*. She thought of Escher's stairways leading nowhere. That Louise Bourgeois print of a young woman cradling an angry-looking baby at the bottom of a staircase to heaven. That night she dreamt of terriers and stray cats falling from the sky. Would she be *furred-in*, rather than snowed in? Limp, sodden bodies piled up against the cinder blocks of the caravan? Waking to sunshine was a relief. She parted the yellow and blue beaded curtain and looked up to the grit-stone moors; the birch trees shimmering like unspoken wishes.

Anne Caldwell

REMNANT

A small wind dropping sand—my father's ash, too refined to be held. A rumination about abstractions of skin and breath; a trestle of air for meditation. After two hours there I'm nearly dissolved. Standing among birds and light and my father is nowhere. Yet a shadow of wind might be an intimation as parcels of his words are blown back. A sense of stubborn eloquence; an insistence on speaking. Digging wind with the sound; claiming an articulate place among all unwieldy indignities. It nudges my own utterance. Though he is dead, yet he will talk.

Paul Hetherington

His old green notebook falls open, seemingly at random. On facing pages—the draft of a poem and its later version, about a quarryman who tapped a block of limestone and eased apart the two halves to reveal the print and cast of a dinosaur footprint. On one page his father buys him a lemonade and the quarryman a pint, then loads the heavy slabs into the Vauxhall's boot. In the next there's his father's empty chair by the stone hearth, a yellow-brown patch on the ceiling.

Paul Munden

ART

Jackson Pollock in his spitting phase. Cheek-fulls of vibrant powder, churned by tongue then hoicked onto canvas, wall, passer-by. The alcohol only for sluicing the bitterness of art from his mouth. It had nothing to do with drinking. It was merely remedial.

Monica Carroll

Countess Gruber had led a rackety life and when the butcher refused her credit she would sell a painting and feast on fillet steaks for weeks. Her soirées were rarely disappointing. She was a magnet for painters who never painted and poets who never wrote. This, naturally, gave them plenty to discuss. There was always a little cocaine at the Gruber parties and she had an excellent cook whom she hadn't paid for years. There were rumours the gardener occasionally slipped into her bed.

Julian Stannard

DOORS

The doors open and close, so many people on the move! My therapist handily deals out a deck of images and then scoops them away: 'What did you see?' I open my eyes and see colour, I close them and see black. Tell me a story? No. He spreads the images out again, palms and fingers splayed to shatter the shapes. I see the curve of shoulder, someone's lovely haunch, an open mouth. The doors open, then close; the black behind my eyes is fading; sometimes a door is just a door.

Jen Webb

She woke crying desolately to find the door open, windows wide and her dream sitting in a chair staring at her. Why do you do this, he asked her, as his black tongue licked his black pudding lips. She thought it a good but obvious question but not one she could answer under pressure of the breaking dawn and the bull roaring in a nearby field. I'm not supposed to have men in my room, she hissed and this was enough to make him run, like all cowards who don't really want the answer. This much she knew.

Jordan Williams

ROOM

Stained concrete steps. He starts to see them in his sleep. But in the morning, when the grey light that passes for day once again takes hold, there they are again, and he has to follow them into the basement gloom, holding a railing of flaking black paint, watching the cockroaches helterskeltering from one stained step to the next. He chooses one of the dungeon rooms and listens to someone talk about teeth, while lichen creeps across the walls. He starts to see teeth in his sleep. He's taken to sleeping now in the dungeon, feeling his own teeth begin to loosen. Tomorrow the clattering cockroaches will be replaced by teeth falling from step to step. The stains will be black, the rooms too dark to find. He won't have the stomach to go on.

Paul Munden

The room is empty. The room is a large black rectangle, blotchy. The heartbeat lifts its hand then does it again.

Owen Bullock

REGRET

For weeks it was nothing but mess. My knitting needles and balls of wool all over the living room, traps for the unwary. Your stacks of magazines, your still smouldering cigarette ends, disasters in waiting. It had to happen, of course. Now we sleepwalk into history, looking back from time to time. Now we puzzle over the principle of regret. Now we acknowledge the truth in a dead man's smile. Put out the moon; it stops the dark escaping.

Jen Webb

He didn't provide. He smacked his daughter one time and bent her finger back. He shared blame for 9/11–the world had not evolved towards peace, he had not evolved.

Owen Bullock

CARE

he turns his hand and brushes the back of it against the back of mine. he lifts his hand then does that again. he reaches up and clasps the seam of my vest between his thumb and fingers. he pulls his hand away. he reaches up and does that again. he watches his hand and separates his fingers. he watches my hand and opens his fist, then closes his fist. he closes his fist around my finger. he opens his hand. he closes his hand around his hand and twists his fingers together. he opens his hand. he rests his hand against my chest. he lifts his hand and then softly he does that again.

Jen Crawford

In that night I held you up in the shower, a grown woman, ill, naked, a broken bowl's shards in your hair. Semi-conscious you leaned against me. I remembered the weight of you, a few weeks old, in my free left hand, as if afloat on fingers; as if magic-carpeted on air. The weight was the same, reaching through my body with love's ceaseless amplitude, crying through fingers as they combed out glass. The shower united us skin to skin, as so often when you were young—lying on your mother's belly in visceral existence; a rumination of light digested by months of days.

Paul Hetherington

OPHELIA

I'm dating Hamlet. He calls me 'whore' when we have sex. It drives me mad but I tell myself he hasn't been himself since his father died. He'll get better with time. I just need to wait patiently and cut him some slack. Last night I took him to Pancake Parlour to cheer him up but he just stabbed at his Long Stack and didn't really eat it. Or the cottage fries we got as a side to share. He spent most of the time on the phone with his mum and left me to pay the bill. I guess he has a lot on his mind. When he dropped me home, I asked him to kiss me goodnight but he said my dad was watching so he backed out of the driveway and did a burnout on our front lawn.

Cassandra Atherton

This is the dress of my drowning. Like pebbles in the pits and pearls in the tide, my colours only sing when submerged. I tack pieces to the toile, worn as I sew, stitching myself in. The fabric is harsh on my hands. Cutting. Each pattern piece a layer of silk under shards of clear diamond, sea sapphire, blood garnet. Every stone gaoled by a silk cross stitch. Amethyst, the tint of lightening at twilight. Emeralds, green as Spring's aggression. My hands milked as I suture my body into heavy beauty. The Haberdasher promised this black-iron buckle the weightiest. I baste it to the waist of gold-laced rick-rack. I tend to shirring on the upper sleeves, puck the gusset underneath, pleat the bodice, so I will fill. Swell. Dark silver braid at the cuffs. Godets inside godets and the skirts are flat felled seamed with sand pressed into the join. Raw edges masked. My collar stays are lead. I will float low to the silt shelf bottom and settle. Shining. Each basted ruby stealing its moment to capture the shifting sun and blaze through black.

Monica Carrollt

BIOGRAPHIES

The Prose Poetry Project (PPP) was created by the International Poetry Studies Institute (IPSI) in November 2014 with the aim of enabling participants to engage in practice-led research into prose poetry and to write prose poems collegially and collaboratively. The project investigates the form and composition of prose poetry and has yielded both creative and research outcomes. It also explores reasons for the resurgence of interest in the prose poem over recent decades. To date, the Project group has members from Australia and the UK, a selection of whom are represented in this anthology.

Cassandra Atherton is an award-winning writer, academic and critic. She has written eight books (with two more in progress) and has been awarded a Harvard Visiting Scholar's position from 2015–2016. http://cassandra-atherton.com

Owen Bullock has published a collection of poetry, *sometimes the sky isn't big enough* (Steele Roberts, 2010), two books of haiku and a novella. He has edited a number of journals, including *Poetry NZ*; and various anthologies, most recently, *Dazzled: The University of Canberra Vice-Chancellor's International Poetry Prize 2014*. Owen is a PhD candidate in Writing at the University of Canberra.

Anne Caldwell is a poet, lecturer in Creative Writing at the University of Bolton in the UK and Deputy Director of the National Association of Writers in Education (NAWE). Her latest poetry collection is *Talking with the*

Dead (Cinnamon, 2011).

Monica Carroll is a writer, poet and post-graduate student at the University of Canberra. Her creative work has been widely awarded and anthologised within Australia and abroad. Her research interests include phenomenology, touch, poetics and space.

Jen Crawford's poetry publications include *Admissions* (Five Islands Press, 2000), *Bad Appendix* (Titus Books, 2008) and *Pop Riveter* (Pania Press, 2011). She is an Assistant Professor of Creative Writing at the University of Canberra, and has also taught in Singapore and New Zealand.

Lucy Dougan's poetry collections are *Memory Shell* (Five Islands Press, 1998); *The Forest Waits: An anthology of poems* (with Andrew Taylor and Kevin Gillam; Southern Forest Arts, 2006); *White Clay* (Giramondo, 2008); *Meanderthals* (Web Del Sol World Voices Chapbooks, 2011) and *Guardians* (Giramondo, 2015). She currently works for the Westerly Centre at the University of Western Australia.

Ross Gibson is Centenary Professor in the Faculty of Arts & Design at the University of Canberra. His books include *26 Views of the Starburst World* (2012), *The Summer Exercises* (2008) and *Seven Versions of an Australian Badland* (2002). His most recent book of poetry *Stone Grown Cold* (2015) is published by Cordite Books.

Paul Hetherington is Head of the International Poetry Studies Institute (IPSI) and Professor of Writing at the University of Canberra. He edited three volumes of the National Library of Australia's four-volume edition of the diaries of the artist Donald Friend and is founding co-editor of the international online journal *Axon: Creative Explorations*. He has published eight full-length poetry collections, most recently *Six Different Windows* (UWA Publishing).

Penelope Layland is a doctoral student in poetry at the University of Canberra. She has published two books of poetry: *The Unlikely Orchard* (Molonglo Books) and *Suburban Anatomy* (Pandanus Books). She has worked as a journalist, speechwriter and as a communications professional.

Andrew Melrose is Professor of Children's Writing at the University of Winchester, UK. He has over 150 film, fiction, non-fiction, research, songs, poems and other writing credits, including *The Story Keepers* film series, a 'textual intervention' on the New Testament, broadcast worldwide, and 33 scholarly or creative books.

Paul Munden is Postdoctoral Research Fellow (Poetry & Creative Practice) at the University of Canberra. He is General Editor of *Writing in Education* and *Writing in Practice*, both published by the National Association of Writers in Education (NAWE), of which he is Director. *Analogue/Digital*, a volume of his new and selected poems, was published this year.

Shane Strange is a doctoral candidate in writing at the University of Canberra where he also tutors and lectures in writing and literary studies. His research interests include creative labour and cultural work; subjectivity and creative practice and cultural representations of the city. He is a writer of essays, short fiction and creative non-fiction and now, prose poetry.

Julian Stannard taught English and American Literature at the University of Genoa and currently teaches English and Creative Writing at the University of Winchester. His most recent collections are *The Street of Perfect Love* (Worple Press, 2014) and *The Parrots of Villa Gruber Discover Lapis Lazuli* (Salmon Poetry, 2011).

Jen Webb is a writer and cultural theorist, and Director of the Centre for Creative and Cultural Research at the University of Canberra. She writes poetry, researches creative practice, and makes and exhibits artist books. Her most recent books are *Watching the World* (with Paul Hetherington) and *Researching Creative Writing.*

Jordan Williams is Associate Professor of Writing at the University of Canberra. She pursues an ongoing interest in the future directions of reading and writing including new forms such as new media writing as well as the growing popularity of older forms such as the graphic novel, and the nexus between fiction and non-fiction.

www.ingramcontent.com/pod-product-compliance
Lightning Source LLC
Chambersburg PA
CBHW020621300426
44113CB00007B/738